D1199425

WE WERE HERE FIRST
THE NATIVE AMERICANS

THE
CHEYENNE

Earle Rice Jr.

PURPLE TOAD

PUBLISHING

WE WERE HERE FIRST
THE NATIVE AMERICANS

Copyright © 2016 by Purple Toad Publishing, Inc.

Printing   1   2   3   4   5   6   7   8   9

PUBLISHER'S NOTE: The data in this book has
been researched in depth, and to the best
of our knowledge is factual. Although every
measure is taken to give an accurate account,
Purple Toad Publishing makes no warranty of
the accuracy of the information and is not
liable for damages caused by inaccuracies.

Publisher's Cataloging-in-Publication Data
Rice, Jr., Earle.
   Cheyenne / written by Earle Rice, Jr.
      p. cm.
      Includes bibliographic references and index.
         ISBN 9781624691669
1. Cheyenne Indians—Juvenile literature. I.
Series: We were here first.
 E99.C53 2016
 978.004973

Library of Congress Control Number:
2015941835

eBook ISBN: 9781624691676

CONTENTS

Colonel John M. Chivington was one of the West's most controversial figures. He was hailed as a hero for repulsing a Confederate force at Glorietta Pass in New Mexico, and called a butcher for ravaging a Cheyenne encampment at Sand Creek, Colorado.

CHAPTER 1
A TIME TO DIE

It was not a good time for the Cheyennes and Arapahos. The Cheyenne-Arapaho War (1864–65) had erupted in the spring of 1864. And U.S. Colonel John M. Chivington, commander of territorial forces in Colorado, had declared war on the regional Indians.

Chivington, a man of massive frame and matching ambition, had won fame as the "Fighting Parson" in 1862. As leader of the First Colorado Cavalry Regiment, the Ohio-born Methodist minister had helped repulse a Confederate invasion force in New Mexico. Two years later, he aspired to political office and saw Indian fighting as a steppingstone to a successful career in politics. In April 1864, he received reports of livestock thefts by a roaming band of Cheyennes. He dispatched elements of the First Colorado with orders to "kill Cheyennes whenever and wherever found."[1]

The first clash between Chivington's cavalry and the Cheyennes came on April 12. Forty troopers led by Lieutenant Clark Dunn intercepted a party of Dog Soldiers along the South Platte River. The Cheyenne warriors were on their way to avenge

Major Jacob Downing

the killing of one of their chiefs by rival Crow warriors. In their travels, they had seized several mules belonging to a white rancher. A skirmish ensued, and both sides suffered several casualties.

Three weeks later, Major Jacob Downing's detachment rode down on a band of Cheyennes camped near Cedar Bluffs, sixty miles above the South Platte. Downing suspected them of stealing cattle and horses. On suspicion only, he launched an attack on twenty-five Cheyennes, destroying their belongings and lodges. In Downing's report, clearly supportive of Chivington's hard-nosed position, he wrote: "I believe now it is but the commencement of war with this tribe, which must result in exterminating them."[2]

On May 16, fifty-four troopers of the Independent Battery of Colorado Volunteer Artillery headed by Lieutenant George Eayre came upon a gathering of hundreds of Sioux and Southern Cheyennes near the Smoky Hill River in western Kansas. The Cheyennes included parties led by Black Kettle and Lean Bear, prominent chiefs who had pledged to keep peace with the whites. They had

Black Kettle

gathered with the Sioux to hunt buffalo for much-needed food.

Upon sighting the soldiers, Lean Bear and a companion rode boldly out to meet them. Lean Bear wore a peace medal on his shirt, presented to him on a recent trip to Washington. In his hand, he carried a paper signed by Abraham Lincoln at that same occasion, attesting to his trustworthiness. When they drew within twenty feet or so of Eayre, the soldiers opened fire. Lean Bear and his companion toppled from their horses. "As they lay on the ground," a Cheyenne witness named Wolf Chief reported later, "the soldiers rode forward and shot them again."[3]

This Cheyenne Chief is believed by many to be Lean Bear.

Furious fighting broke out. The soldiers opened fire with two mountain howitzers, pummeling the Indians with grapeshot. Both sides took on numerous casualties in the brief but intense confrontation. Eayre reported two dozen warriors killed. Black Kettle, always an advocate for peace with the whites, rode forward to end the fighting. "He told us we must not fight with the white people," said Wolf Chief, "so we stopped."[4]

The killing of Lean Bear touched off an Indian rampage

Mountain Howitzer

that lasted all summer. Cheyenne, Arapaho, and Kiowa warriors banded together and killed dozens of white settlers and travelers. In a campaign of death and destruction, they effectively isolated the Colorado Territory and emerging town of Denver from all freight and mail delivery.

Territorial governor John Evans viewed the regional tribes as obstacles to further settlement and his own political aims. He hoped to become United States senator when Colorado achieved statehood. When he failed to persuade the regional Indians to move onto a small, inadequate reservation below Sand Creek, southeast of Denver, he stirred up fears of an Indian uprising aimed at driving the whites from the area.

After receiving a false report that Indians were approaching town, Evans issued a proclamation authorizing citizens "to kill and destroy, as enemies of the country, all such hostile Indians."[5] In multiple telegrams to Washington, he appealed for reinforcements, predicting the "largest Indian war this country has ever had."[6]

On August 13, the War Department granted Evans permission to recruit another regiment—the Third Colorado Cavalry. Its members were authorized to serve for one hundred days. Their limited service earned them the nickname of the "Hundred Dazers." Unlike regular army regiments, the Third Colorado's sole purpose was to fight Indians. Its ranks consisted largely of rowdies and toughs from mining camps and Denver saloons.

On September 28, encouraged by Major Edward Wynkoop, the sympathetic commander of Fort Lyon in southeastern Colorado, Black Kettle and his followers met with Governor Evans. Appealing to the governor, Black Kettle said, "All we ask is that we may have peace with the whites."[7] Evans evaded the chief's sincerity. In private, he told Wynkoop that the Third Colorado was being "raised to kill Indians, and they must kill Indians."[8]

At the close of the meeting, Colonel Chivington unwittingly provided Black Kettle and his group with what they were seeking. "My rule of fighting white men or Indians is to fight them until they lay down their arms and submit to military authority,"[9] he said. He advised them to surrender to Wynkoop at Fort Lyon. Black Kettle took him at his word. The Cheyenne and

Front row, kneeling, left to right: Major Edward W. Wynkoop; Captain Silas S. Soule. Middle row, left to right: possibly White Antelope, Bull Bear, Black Kettle, One Eye, Natame (Arapaho). Back row: Two unnamed men, John H. Smith (interpreter), Heap of Buffalo (Arapaho), Neva (Arapaho), unknown man, sentry.

Arapaho settled in at Sand Creek, near the fort. They believed they had abided by Chivington's rule and were at peace with the white man.

Near the end of November, Chivington and the Third Colorado gathered at Fort Lyon. At dawn on November 29, Chivington and the Hundred Dazers—seven hundred mounted men and a battery of four twelve-pound howitzers—attacked the Indian encampment at Sand Creek. The crazed soldiers—many of them drunk—charged the camp of some six hundred Cheyennes and fifty Arapahos, committing unspeakable atrocities and

The Sand Creek Massacre by artist Robert Lindneaux. In an attack lasting eight hours, nearly 700 volunteer soldiers led by Colonel John M. Chivington killed about 200 peaceful Cheyenne and Arapaho people, most of them women, children, and the elderly.

killing anything that moved. Many Indians escaped the bloodbath, including Black Kettle, but at least two hundred Indians lay dead and mutilated when the fighting ended.

It was not a good time for the Cheyennes and Arapahos. It was a time to die.

Dog Soldiers

Most tribes of Plains Indians were organized into fraternal, military, and religious societies or orders. The Cheyenne, distinguished for their warlike qualities, originally formed five military societies—the Dog, Fox, Elk, Shield, and Bowstring. They later added the Wolf and the Northern Crazy Dogs. Each society had its own special dances, songs, medicine bundles, and costumes. These elite warriors kept law and order within the tribe and led the other warriors in battle.

Cheyenne Dog Soldier

Among these military orders, the *Hotamitaneo*, or Dog Society Men, was far and away the most renowned. Popularly known as Dog Soldiers—so named by the U.S. military—its members were chosen for their bravery and warrior skills. Membership was considered an honor and earned a warrior great respect.

Dog Soldiers wore a sash of tanned skin, about eight to ten feet long and five or six inches wide. It was called a dog-rope. In battle, a selected warrior would ride ahead of the others, dismount, and drive a lance through the sash. Anchored in place, he would stay there throughout the fighting, battling the enemy and urging the others into the fray—a cheerleader of sorts in a deadly game. Honor bound to remain at his position until released by his companions, the warrior often died on the spot.

Though other Plains tribes also had Dog Soldiers, the Cheyenne *Hotamitaneo* fought with such fury and daring that the name was most often taken to mean only them.

Chief Wolf Robe, of the Southern Cheyenne, was a recipient of the Benjamin Harrison Peace Medal. Photographs of Wolf Robe have served as a subject for numerous artists and sculptors. Some believe he was the model for the profile on the Indian Head Nickel.

CHAPTER 2
GETTING TO KNOW THE CHEYENNE

History has recorded the Cheyenne as one of the most prominent tribes of all the Plains Indians. Few people think of them as woodland Indians, but they trace their roots back to the Great Lakes region in territory now known as Minnesota. They are Algonquin-speaking people and call themselves Tsistsistas, meaning "beautiful people." The Sioux, who spoke a different language, named them Cheyenne (pronounced shy-ANN), which means "red talkers"—those who speak a foreign tongue—or "people of a different speech." That is the name by which the world has come to know them.

The word *Cheyenne* was once thought to come from *chien*—the French word for "dog"—because of its seeming relation to the Dog Soldiers. That possible derivation has been thoroughly discounted in favor of the foregoing explanation.

Scholars traditionally divide Cheyenne history into four stages or periods. Originally, the Cheyenne resided in the upper Mississippi Valley. In the sixteenth and seventeenth centuries, they moved north to Minnesota and established permanent earth-lodge villages. There they lived the sedentary life of agricultural people, planting corn and beans.

Pressured by the westward migration of the Sioux—who in turn were pressured by the Ojibway—the Cheyenne moved

During the "time of the buffalo," the Cheyenne lived near the Missouri River and the Black Hills.

northwest to the Sheyenne River in North Dakota. Wolf dogs traveled with them. Accordingly, their second stage is sometimes called the "time of the dogs." They continued to grow corn and beans and maintain a stationary lifestyle.

About 1750, the Cheyenne acquired horses and migrated first into the Missouri River country and later into the game lands of the Black Hills. There they assimilated the Suhtai people and allied themselves with the Arapaho, both Algonquin-speaking tribes. This move marked the beginning of their life on the Plains as hunters and followers of the buffalo. For obvious reasons, this stage is sometimes referred to as the "time of the buffalo." It was a period of plenty.

The fourth stage is the reservation phase, which will be discussed later.

In the early 1830s, a large group of Cheyennes settled on the upper Arkansas River to avail themselves of trade facilities offered by the newly built Bent's Fort. The Cheyennes began separating into northern and southern groups. "This split soon became so profound that within a few decades, the Northern and Southern Cheyennes became two distinct nations," writes Western historian Charles M. Robinson III. "Although friendly contact remained, by 1860 their history becomes totally separate."[1]

At the same time, both branches of the Cheyennes retained close ties. "The Cheyenne people," as noted by scholars Rubie Sootkis, a Northern Cheyenne, and Terry Straus, "had sustained (and continue to sustain) linguistic, cultural, and spiritual bonds through continual visits and joint ceremonial activities, and think of themselves as kin who share a common cultural tradition."[2]

In the north, the Cheyennes fought with the Sioux for a time and eventually allied with them. Similarly, their counterparts in the south first made war against the Kiowas and Comanches, then loosely allied with them to fight against the Crows, Pawnees, Shoshones, Utes, and Apaches. Both Cheyenne factions continued their alliance with the Arapahos, now separated into northern and southern divisions.

Despite their separation, the new lifestyle of the Cheyennes—in "the classic horse-buffalo-tipi complex of the high plains"[3]—remained virtually the same. The horse changed their lifestyle dramatically. With their shift from the near-stationary woodland existence to the highly mobile Plains life, they left their earth-lodge dwellings behind and adopted the portable tipi (or tepee). Tipis could be collapsed and moved in an hour or two. The Cheyennes' largely vegetarian diet gave way to a staple of meat from the buffalo, which also provided skins from which they built tipis.

On the Plains, the Cheyenne retained some of their heritage but in many ways essentially reinvented themselves. In the Cheyenne culture, the most important unit is the family, followed by the band, and finally by the tribe. The tribe consisted of ten bands. By the time the Cheyenne had reached the Plains, they had formed a "Council of Forty-Four" to govern their nation. It was made up of four chiefs from each band and four principals. The latter were elder chiefs who had previously served on the council with distinction.

Council chiefs were known for their wisdom and fairness. They ruled on day-to-day matters affecting the tribe, such as settling disputes and

These Cheyenne tipis are typical of the easily collapsible and transportable dwellings used by the Plains Indians.

Cheyenne Chief White
Buffalo

deciding when to move to another campsite. The council used the force of its moral authority to keep the peace both inside and outside the tribe. Council chiefs also made decisions about alliances and war policy. In matters of specific raids or strategic details, however, they generally deferred to the soldier societies. Chiefs of individual bands were responsible for decisions affecting members of their own bands.

Above all, the family served as the building block for the Cheyenne social organization. Men were the hunters and warriors. They provided food and protection for their families. Women ran the home. Their responsibilities included cooking, cleaning, and making the family's clothing. They also built the tipis out of buffalo skins and wooden poles, erecting, dismantling, and moving them as needed.

Young children played games with toys suitable to their future roles in the tribe. Girls "played house" with dolls and little tipis. Boys prepared for battles still to come with small bows, arrows, shields, and lances. As children grew older, they began to learn the skills of their parents. All Cheyenne children became expert riders. Girls carried water and gathered wood and buffalo chips for the fire. They learned how to tan skins, sew clothing, dry meat, make pemmican, build tipis, and prepare for marriage. And they learned how to defend themselves using a knife or bow and arrows. Boys went hunting with their fathers, learned how to make hunting gear and weapons, and practiced their horsemanship. In leisure hours, they listened to elders recount the history and traditions of their people.

Perhaps no stories have been told more than the Cheyenne creation myth and the legend of Sweet Medicine.

The Things They Wore

Men's shirt

Though the buffalo lent its hide to Cheyenne tipis, the Cheyenne turned to the softer skins of deer, antelope, and mountain sheep for most of their clothes. Men's early clothing consisted simply of skins tied on with thongs. They wore no shirts until the whites came. Later, they wore breechcloths with leather leggings. On the Plains, they adopted the war shirt and wore it long, almost to the knees. They often decorated their clothing with buttons, shells, and deer hooves.

Early on, Cheyenne women wore the "strap-and-sleeve" dress. It consisted of two rectangular pieces of skin, tied together with thongs at intervals down the sides. Later, they wore long, fringed deerskin dresses, abundantly beaded and decorated with animal teeth and fancy quillwork. A single dress could weigh as much as twelve pounds.

Women's dress

Both Cheyenne men and women wore their hair braided. Women sometimes wore their hair loose and flowing. On occasion, men wore the halo war bonnet. Distinguished warriors wore the buffalo-horn headdress. Men's footwear consisted of leather moccasins with rawhide soles, adorned with beading or quillwork. Women wore "boots," a combination of moccasins and leggings, decorated with fringe and lazy stitch beadwork.

Both genders wore robes of tanned deer, elk, antelope, or buffalo hide. Like other Plains tribes, Cheyennes highly valued robes of the white buffalo, whose color varied from dusty gray to pale cream.

Halo War Bonnet

In the Cheyenne creation myth, the god Maheo gave the snow goose and the loon the gift of flight. When they grew tired of flying, Maheo created land on which they could build their nests.

CHAPTER 3
MAHEO AND SWEET MEDICINE

The Cheyenne believed in an all-Spirit named Maheo, who lived alone in a dark void. In time, he grew lonely and decided to create a world. First, with his amazing power, he created a great salty lake. Then he created fish and other water beings. Next, he created snow geese, mallards, teal, coots, terns, and loons to live on the water's surface.

So that he could see his creations better, Maheo created light. It was then that a snow goose came to him. It explained how birds differed from fish, and how they sometimes grew tired of swimming. Maheo listened and gave the birds the gift of flight. But soon a loon came to him and said the birds were tired of swimming and flying. They needed land on which to build their nests. Maheo said he needed help to create land from mud at the bottom of the lake.

Most of the birds flew high into the sky and then tried to dive to the lake's bottom for mud. But they all failed to reach bottom. Then a little coot swam by and volunteered to help. The coot dove toward the bottom of the lake. It was gone for a long, long time. Finally, the little coot returned to the surface and placed a ball of mud into Maheo's hand. Maheo looked all about for somewhere to put the mud but could not find a suitable place. None of the water creatures had the surface he needed.

Maheo built the earth on the back of Grandmother Turtle.

Then Grandmother Turtle arrived.

Maheo packed the ball of mud on Grandmother Turtle's back to carry, and he began to create earth. First, he added grass, flowers, and trees to the mud. Next, he pulled out one of his ribs and created the first man on earth. When Grandmother Turtle advised him that the man would be lonely all by himself, Maheo pulled out a left rib and created the first woman.

Maheo now sat back and thought about his creations. He recognized their needs and gave them the gift of the buffalo to provide them with food, warmth, and clothing. Because the animals helped Maheo, the Cheyenne

Buffalo

have forever after respected the spirits of animals and their part in creating the rest of the world.

Cheyenne religion recognizes numerous gods. Maheo is the creator of all physical and spiritual life in *Hestanov,* the Cheyenne universe. Cheyennes know him variously as their Divine God, Divine Creator, Great Spirit, or the Wise One Above. Cheyenne religion is complicated and based largely on four sacred ceremonies revealed to them by Sweet Medicine.

"Before his birth the people were bad, living without law and killing one another," writes Cheyenne historian John Stands in Timber. "But with his life those things changed. Indians are often called savages, and it was true of the Cheyennes at first, but not after Sweet Medicine time."[1]

Sweet Medicine—or Motzeyout—was the legendary prophet and savior of the Cheyenne. Because early Cheyenne history was handed down through the ages orally, accounts of his origin are unclear and vary with the telling. One version of Sweet Medicine's legend tells that he was held in his mother's womb for four

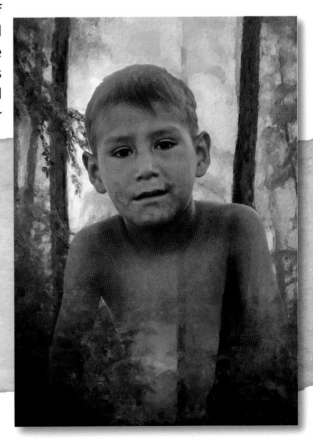

In Cheyenne lore, Arrow Boy's mother carried him in her womb for four years before giving birth. Arrow Boy grew up quickly and ran away from his tribe. In a mountain cavern, he spent fours years among the gods, learning the arts of the medicine men.

years and born with supernatural powers. In his boyhood, he was known as Arrow Boy.

Arrow Boy learned and grew quickly. Even in his youth, he showed his people great magic and imparted much knowledge. One day he went hunting with children of the tribe and killed his first calf. An old man came upon him while he was skinning the calf. He tried to yank it away from Arrow Boy, but Arrow Boy hit him over the head and knocked him out. The other children ran back to the village to tell about the incident. Arrow Boy, angry now, cast a curse upon the tribe, calling a famine down on it. Then he ran away.

Arrow Boy disappeared for a long time. Legend has it that he seemed to be called by a great power and traveled a long way to the Black Hills country.

Noahvose, the mountain sacred to the Cheyenne, rises in the distance. The mountain, now called Bear Butte, is located near Sturgis, South Dakota. Many Native Americans make pilgrimages to the mountain and leave prayer cloths and tobacco bundles tied to the branches of trees along its flanks.

He finally reached a mountain known ever after by the Cheyenne as Noahvose, or Sacred Mountain. Today, it is called Bear Butte.

Arrow Boy found an opening in the mountain and entered an area like a big lodge or tipi. A line of old men and women sat on opposite sides, but they were not people, they were gods. "The old ones called him Grandson and began instructing him in many things he should take back to the people," writes John Stands in Timber. "They taught him first about the arrows, because they were to be the highest power in the tribe. Two were for hunting and two for war. Many ceremonies were connected with them, and they stood for many laws. He was taught the ceremony of renewing the arrows, which must take place if one Cheyenne killed another."[2]

According to John Stands in Timber, he next learned "that he was to give the people a good government, with forty-four chiefs to manage it, and a good system of police and military protection."[3] There was so much more to teach Arrow Boy, the old ones kept him at Noahvose for the next four years.

When Arrow Boy returned to the tribe as Sweet Medicine, he lifted the curse of famine from the Cheyenne. In a double tipi, he organized a government of forty-four chiefs and established the military societies. Then he taught the chiefs their duties and how they were to be chosen.

A Cheyenne chief with war paint and a buffalo horn bonnet. Only distinguished warriors wore this kind of headdress.

"At last he taught them the principles of the Arrow religion: how the Arrows were to be referenced and cared for and used for the betterment of the people,"[4] writes John Stands in Timber. (See "Cheyenne Ceremonies," next page.)

Sweet Medicine lived a long life and guided his people along a peaceful path for many years. He died in a small hut near Noahvose, the Sacred Mountain. With his last words, he foretold the coming of the white man and appealed to his people to be strong.

This lone tipi in the wilderness seems to reflect a long-past era of serenity when Native Americans lived in harmony with nature. Sweet Medicine foretold of the white man's coming and the changes he would bring.

Cheyenne Ceremonies

Cheyenne religion largely centered on four major ceremonies. They were the renewal of the Sacred Arrows, or *Mahuts*; the Sacred Buffalo Hat, or *Esevone*; the New Life Lodge, or Sun Dance (*Hoxeheome*); and the Animal Dance, or *Massaum*.

To the Cheyenne, the Sacred Arrows are living things. They consider them their holiest tribal possessions. The gods presented them in a bundle to Sweet Medicine—two "man arrows" for warfare and two "bison arrows" for hunting. Through the Sacred Arrows, Maheo pours his life into the lives of the Cheyenne people, and they remain one with him. The annual renewal ritual is performed by males only—to renew the arrows, to renew the tribe, and to empower the men.

Cheyenne Animal Dancers

The Sacred Buffalo Hat was a gift from Maheo to the Suhtai prophet Erect Horns (Tomsivi). Its power is female. When it is renewed, the keeper of the Hat prays and offers a pipe to Maheo, the Earth, and the Four Directions (gods). Maheo assures continual life and blessings for the people.

Cheyennes performed the Sun Dance to praise Maheo for the creation of Earth and the universe. The annual dance also celebrated all the spirits and the renewal of life.

In the Animal Dance, men dressed as animals, and members of the Bowstring Society pretended to hunt them. The ritual was thought to bring success to the hunters.

In his westward expansion, the white man brought with him guns and a lust for land. This painting called *Through the Smoke Sprang the Daring Soldier* (1897) shows U.S. soldiers in an attack on the Northern Cheyenne.

CHAPTER 4
THE CHEYENNE WAY

Sweet Medicine lived among the Cheyenne for many years. He taught them how to live properly in a world where life was hard. Before he died in the shadow of Bear Butte, he left his people with a warning of things to come:

> [S]ome time after I am dead . . . light-skinned bearded men will arrive with sticks spitting fire. They will conquer the land and drive you before them. They will kill the animals who give you their flesh that you may live, and they will bring strange animals for you to ride and eat. They will introduce war and evil, strange sickness and death.[1]

Sweet Medicine also warned that the newcomers would try to make them forget Maheo. He called on the Cheyenne to be strong, lest they perish from the earth. But he had also taught them to be generous and caring. So, at first, the Cheyenne welcomed the light-skinned strangers as friends, and kept the peace well into the first half of the nineteenth century.

The wagons were packed full with everything from basic necessities to a family's most treasured possessions. Heavy items often had to be abandoned along the trail.

The canvas top was supported by a frame of bowed wood. The ends could be closed with a drawstring in bad weather.

Teams of mules or oxen pulled the heavy wagons.

Wagons were constructed mostly of wood and with a minimum of metal parts in order to keep them lightweight.

The wooden wheels were rimmed in iron to prevent wear.

White settlers crossed the Oregon Trail using sturdy wagons. The wagons had to be strong enough to endure 2,000 miles of jolting wilderness, yet light enough for the mules or oxen to pull them.

In 1825, the Cheyenne signed the Friendship Treaty to establish their first formal relations with the U.S. government. Cheyenne-White relations remained cordial until the 1840s. During this decade, a surge of white settlers migrating along the Oregon Trail brought diseases, mistreated the environment, and harmed buffalo herds. The Cheyenne and their allies met the intrusions with a series of minor raids.

To end Indian hostilities with the whites and between themselves, the U.S. government negotiated the Treaty of 1851. The Cheyenne and eight other tribes agreed to grant westbound travelers safe passage in return for goods worth $50,000 each year for fifty years. Peace prevailed for a while, but the treaty soon fell apart under the pressure of tribal rivalry, shifting Plains societies, and the incessant flow of emigrating Americans.

The loss of Cheyenne land, bit by bit, the disappearance of the buffalo, and the construction of fort after fort by the advancing Americans finally forced the Cheyenne to fight. They waged war off and on against the whites for the next twenty-five years. The whites returned the assaults fiercely. In battling the whites, the Cheyenne probably lost more than any other Plains tribe in proportion to their numbers.

Disease took a further toll on the Cheyenne. They suffered terribly from a cholera outbreak in 1849, which nearly wiped out several bands. An estimated 2,000 souls died, or about two-thirds of their numbers before the epidemic.

After sporadic raids in the mid-1850s, the Cheyenne generally sued for peace in the summer of 1858. They remained peaceful for the most part until provoked by Colonel Chivington's brutal raid on Black Kettle's camp at Sand Creek in 1864.

In 1868, General Phil Sheridan launched a winter campaign against the Indians camped on the Canadian and Washita rivers in Indian Territory (now Oklahoma). In the early morning hours of November 27, 1868, a column of cavalry led by Lieutenant Colonel George A. Custer—the "boy general" of Civil War fame—attacked a sleeping village of Cheyenne and Arapaho on the Washita River. Unknown to Custer, it was the village of Black Kettle, the peace-seeking Cheyenne chief who had survived Chivington's raid at Sand Creek. Custer's troops killed 103 Indians, 93 of whom were

George A. Custer

29

Lieutenant Colonel George Armstrong Custer and his Seventh Cavalry attacked the sleeping village of Cheyenne Chief Black Kettle. They slew 103 villagers, mostly women, children, and old men.

women, children, and old men. Black Kettle and his wife leaped on a pony and tried to escape the galloping cavalrymen.

"At the river a bullet slammed into Black Kettle's back, and another struck his wife," wrote Western historian Robert M. Utley. "Together they fell into the icy stream, dead."[2] Black Kettle's luck had run out. Eight years later, the Cheyenne and Arapaho, along with a large body of Sioux, met Custer again at another river—the Little Bighorn.

Late in the spring of 1876, General Sheridan launched another campaign against the Indians, this time in the northern plains. He sent three columns into the Sioux country of what is now southeastern Montana. Some 1,500 Sioux and Cheyenne warriors met the first column of about 1,200 cavalry led by General George Crook at the Rosebud River. In six hours of furious fighting, the Indians battled Crook's troopers to a draw, and Crook retreated. Meanwhile, the other two army columns had taken the field in Montana.

Some 600 troopers of the Seventh Cavalry led by Lieutenant Colonel George A. Custer reached the Little Bighorn about noon on June 25. Across the river stood a camp of about 6,000 Sioux and Cheyenne, a third of whom were men and boys of fighting age. In the battle that ensued, in the words of Robert M. Utley, "George Armstrong Custer presided over one of the most complete disasters in American military annals."[3] In all, 263 officers, troopers, scouts, and civilians, and about 50 Indians, died along the Little Bighorn River. It was the Indians' greatest victory of the Indian Wars.

The third column led by General Alfred Terry and Colonel John Gibbon arrived the next day, but the Indians had already moved on. Though the Indians won a great battle at the Little Bighorn, they had lost the war. More battles lay ahead, but Congress approved more soldiers, and the Indian Wars drew to a close.

Custer's Last Stand

The Southern Cheyenne surrendered in 1875 and were settled into a reservation in Indian Territory (Oklahoma), but the Northern Cheyenne fought on until 1879. Among the Cheyenne, as George Bird Grinnell wrote long ago, "The fighting spirit was encouraged. . . . How much better . . . to struggle and fight, to be brave and accomplish great things, to receive the respect and applause of everyone in the camp, and finally to die gloriously at the hands of the enemy!"[4] It was the Cheyenne way.

But all people have limits.

In 1877, the U.S. government forced some one thousand Northern Cheyenne to march to Indian Territory and join their southern brethren in the reservation. The northerners found conditions there intolerably hot. They felt culturally alienated, and many starved. Others were infected with measles, dysentery, and malaria.

In the autumn of 1878, more than three hundred Northern Cheyenne led by Chiefs Dull Knife and Little Wolf fled the reservation and headed north on a fifteen-hundred-mile flight to freedom.

Cheyenne chiefs Dull Knife (left) and Little Wolf led their people in a northward flight from the Southern Cheyenne Reservation. Author Mari Sandoz immortalized their story in *Cheyenne Autumn.*

Long Way Home

Prisoners who were with Dull Knife

The Cheyenne chiefs Dull Knife and Little Wolf feared that their tribe would die out in the inhospitable conditions of the southern reservation. They pleaded for a reservation for their people in their former home territory. When their pleas went unanswered, they acted on their own.

On September 9, 1878, the two chiefs led a band of eighty-nine warriors and 246 women and children on a fifteen-hundred-mile trek to their northern homelands. Their tragic story was later memorialized in Mari Sandoz's novel *Cheyenne Autumn* and John Ford's film of the same name.

Soldiers pursued fleeing Cheyenne, killing many of them along the way. After crossing the South Platte River, the Cheyenne split into two bands. Little Wolf's band made it safely back to Montana. Army troops eventually captured Dull Knife's band and escorted them to Fort Robinson in Nebraska—setting the conditions for what came to be known as the Fort Robinson Massacre.

On January 3, 1879, government authorities ordered the return of Dull Knife's band to the Southern Cheyenne reservation. "Driven by desperation and hunger," writes Charles M. Robinson III, "they broke out on January 9, 1879. Sixty-five were rounded up and brought back by morning, along with the bodies of fifty who, weakened by starvation and exposure, had died during the night. Ultimately most were captured."[5]

After their autumn of despair and winter of devastation, the Northern Cheyenne finally received their own reservation in Montana in 1884.

Against a snowy background, horses cross the highway in the Northern Cheyenne Reservation. Horses brought a whole new way of life to the Cheyenne and still fill an important role in the lives of many.

CHAPTER 5
STILL CHEYENNE

In 1884, the Tongue River Indian Reservation was established by executive order in southeastern Montana, but it was not exclusively granted to the Northern Cheyenne. A further executive order in 1900 granted the reservation to the tribe. The same order renamed it the Northern Cheyenne Indian Reservation and expanded it to its present boundaries. Today, the Northern Cheyenne Tribe of the Northern Cheyenne Reservation is a federally recognized tribe with its own constitution as an IRA (Indian Reorganization Act) tribe.

The reservation currently encompasses 440,000 acres of land in the rugged Montana countryside. It is bounded in the west by the Crow Reservation and in the east by the Tongue River. Some 5,000 Northern Cheyenne live on the reservation, as well as members of other tribes, along with non-Native Americans. There are approximately 10,800 enrolled tribal members. Lame Deer, one of five districts on the reservation, serves as the tribal and government agency headquarters.

The tribe's constitution and by-laws designate a tribal government consisting of an elected president, vice president, and sergeant-at-arms; the appointed offices of treasurer and secretary; and ten tribal council members, elected from the five districts for four-year staggered terms. It also provides for three branches of tribal government: the executive (president, vice president, treasurer, and secretary), legislative (tribal council), and judicial (designated courts).

Major employers on the reservation include the St. Labre Indian School in Ashland, the federal government, the tribal government, and power and construction companies. Farming, logging, ranching, and small businesses help support the Northern Cheyenne economy. Several small textile factories and a casino also contribute.

Despite these industries, the unemployment rate fluctuates between 60 and 75 percent, depending on seasonal employment. On average, reservation income stagnates at poverty levels. Those not familiar with the Cheyenne culture might question why the reservation dwellers do not leave the reservation to seek employment elsewhere. The reasons are varied, as outlined in *We, The Northern Cheyenne People*, published by the Chief Dull Knife College in Lame Deer:

> They love their land. They stay to be with their families and so their children can benefit from time spent with family elders. They participate in tribal traditional and religious activities. They get more medical and economic benefits from the federal and tribal governments than members who live elsewhere. Many feel strongly that they want to serve their people and often leave to complete their education, later returning to work. It is the only place where they can expect to hear and speak their language and be surrounded by people of their culture. Many of their ancestors are buried there.[1]

Ironically, their reservation sits atop rich coal deposits that could be exploited and provide a profusion of much-needed jobs. "The Tribe has an abundance of natural resources on its homeland in southeastern Montana and it has fought to keep these resources undeveloped for generations," notes writer Alexis Bonogofsky of the National Wildlife Federation. "Because the Tribe has invested countless hours and resources in protecting tribal lands, the Northern Cheyenne reservation maintains clean water, clean air and pristine wildlife habitat."[2] Multinational coal companies continue to pressure the tribe to open their lands to coal mining. How long the tribe can resist corporate pressures remains an open question.

The tribe's efforts to preserve its lands and environment extended to its cultural heritage. Northern Cheyennes maintain cultural and spiritual ties with their southern cousins by holding ceremonies such as the Sun Dance, renewal of the Sacred Arrows, and the Sacred Buffalo (or Medicine) Hat. (The Animal Dance is no longer practiced.) Members of each tribe often travel long distances to attend rituals staged by the other.

Today's Southern Cheyenne—now officially named just Cheyenne—moved to the Indian Territory (Oklahoma) as a result of the Medicine Lodge Treaty of 1867. In 1869, an executive order set aside lands for the Cheyenne and Arapaho tribes on the north fork of the Canadian River.

Acting under the provisions of the Dawes (Allotment) Act of 1887, the government allotted a small portion of reservation land to each Indian and sold most of the rest of the land to settlers. In 1892, the Oklahoma Land Run

Medicine Lodge
Peace Council

opened the Cheyenne-Arapaho Reservation lands for settlement by homesteaders in what was now the U.S. state of Oklahoma. The Indians retained only a small portion of their original lands. (Northern Cheyenne tribal members were allotted 160 acres each in the early 1930s. Their reservation lands were never opened for white homesteading.)

The (Southern) Cheyenne now form a part of the federally recognized Cheyenne-Arapaho tribe. After the Indian Welfare Act of 1936, the tribes formed their own government. Its headquarters is located in a complex of buildings in Concho, a small town north of El Reno. The tribe is governed by a Tribal Council made up of all tribal members eighteen and older, plus executive, legislative, and judicial branches, and a tribal court.

Three Cheyenne chiefs enjoy themselves at a Red Earth parade. In the Annual Red Earth Native American Cultural Festival, North American Indian artists and dancers celebrate their rich diversity.

Students from the Cheyenne and Arapaho Tribal College educate young people to remember their heritage.

As of 2014, the Cheyenne-Arapaho tribe numbered some 12,000 enrolled citizens. About 8,000 of those consider themselves Cheyenne. The tribe owns more than 10,500 acres, spread across eight counties in western Oklahoma. It also holds jurisdiction over some 70,000 acres of individual allotments. Most tribal members no longer reside on the reservation. Instead, they live on tribal trust lands in the western part of the state. (Lands held "in trust" by the federal government are exempt from state and county taxes. They can be sold only in accordance with federal regulations.)

Farming and ranching, oil exploitation, and government programs provide the main source of income for the Cheyenne, but unemployment figures—like those of their northern cousins—run high among them. Smoke shops, bingo halls, casinos, and recreational businesses scattered around the trust lands add to Cheyenne incomes, but life remains an ongoing challenge for many Cheyenne. Despite these challenges, the Cheyenne spirit remains indomitable.

Flag of the Northern Cheyenne and (right) emblem for the Southern Cheyenne and Arapaho Tribes today.

"We started out with 51 million acres and we ended up with 160 acres," remarked Cheyenne Chief Laird Cometsevah. "But through all this, we are still Cheyenne and they will never take that away from us."[3]

Northern Cheyenne Reservation land

The Last Battle

A bike rider cycles past the sprawling Coalstrip power plant near Lame Deer.

Traditionally, the Cheyenne have linked their way of life—their religion, culture, and very existence—to the pristine purity of its land, air, and water. They believe they are one with Mother Earth. Though rich coal deposits lie beneath the buttes of their northern reservation, the Cheyenne have rejected the development of coal for decades. But now, jobs are scarce and poverty is pervasive on the reservation. And coal holds the promise of employment and good wages.

The Northern Cheyenne Indian Reservation stands as a house divided. One faction of the tribe wants to mine coal or dig wells to extract methane gas from the coal. Leroy Spang, tribal leader and proponent of economic self-sufficiency, declared, "Today we advocate for the sound development of our resources. We know that with development comes jobs, businesses, infrastructure improvement, and the promise of a future."[4]

Opponents of coal development fear the erosion of tribal traditions. Ted Risingsun, cultural leader and tribal council member, denounced the promise of greater employment and economic development. "I think I would rather be poor in my own country," he said, "with my own people, with our own way of life than be rich in a torn-up land where I am outnumbered ten to one by strangers."[5]

The debate rages on. Perhaps the last battle the "Fighting Cheyennes" will ever fight will be their struggle to preserve their lands and environment from the exploitation of coal and gas corporations.

- Cheyenne couples typically had between one and three children.
- After the Cheyenne acquired the horse, their diet changed from vegetables to buffalo meat, supplemented by fruits, nuts, berries, and fish.
- The Cheyenne used sign language to communicate with other local tribes. Today, most tribal members speak English.
- Cheyenne warriors engaged in "counting coup." A "coup" was defined as such acts as touching a live enemy with the hand, killing or scalping an enemy, stealing an enemy's horse, touching an enemy's tipi, and more. "Counting coup" referred to a public recitation of such deeds of valor. *Coup* is French for "a blow delivered in combat."
- The biggest enemy of the Cheyenne were the Pawnee, because they tried to steal Cheyenne lands. The Cheyenne also feared the Kiowa and Crow tribes, and ghosts.
- Cheyenne crafts included beadwork, deer-skin dolls, bracelets, and sleds made from buffalo ribs, and they excelled at making pottery.
- The Cheyenne played a popular game called Hoop and Pole, in which a hoop or ring is rolled along the ground as a target for arrows or lances.
- Cheyenne warriors ranged as far south as Mexico, once losing three men in a fight with Mexican lancers in 1853.
- Today, the Cheyenne are involved in the Native American Church (or peyote religion), as well as Christian denominations, particularly the Catholic Church in Montana and the Mennonite Church on both reservations.

Chapter 1

1. Editors of Time-Life Books, *War for the Plains.* The American Indians series (Alexandria, VA: Time-Life Books, 1994), p. 79.

2. Ibid., p. 80.

3. George Bird Grinnell, *The Fighting Cheyennes* (North Deighton, MA: JG Press, 1995), p. 140.

4. Ibid.

5. Editors of Time-Life Books, *War for the Plains,* p. 82.

6. Ibid.

7. Ibid., p. 85.

8. Alan Axelrod, *Chronicle of the Indian Wars: From Colonial Times to Wounded Knee* (New York: Prentice Hall General Reference, 1993), p. 196.

9. Robert M. Utley, *The Indian Frontier of the American West 1846–1890* (Albuquerque: University of New Mexico Press, 1993), p. 91.

Chapter 2

1. Charles M. Robinson III, *A Good Year to Die: The Story of the Great Sioux War* (New York: Random House, 1995), p. 7.

2. Rubie Sootkis and Terry Straus, "Northern Cheyenne," in *Encyclopedia of North American Indians,* edited by Frederick E. Hoxie (Boston: Houghton Mifflin Company, 1996), p. 111.

3. Ibid., p. 110.

Chapter 3

1. John Stands in Timber, "Cheyenne Memories," 2011, http://www.cheyennenation.com/memories.html

2. Ibid.

3. Ibid.

4. Ibid.

Chapter 4

1. Anti-Defamation League, "The Cheyenne Way of Peace: Sweet Medicine," http://archive.adl.org/education/curriculum_connections/cheyenne_way.html

2. Robert M. Utley, *The Indian Frontier of the American West 1846–1890* (Albuquerque: University of New Mexico Press, 1993), p. 127.

3. Ibid., p. 184.

4. George Bird Grinnell, *The Fighting Cheyennes* (North Deighton, MA: JG Press, 1995), p. 9.

5. Charles M. Robinson III, *A Good Year to Die: The Story of the Great Sioux War* (New York: Random House, 1995), p. 341.

Chapter 5

1. Chief Dull Knife College, *We, The Northern Cheyenne People: Our Land, Our History, Our Culture* (Lame Deer, MT: Chief Dull Knife College, 2008), p. 147.

2. Alexis Bonogofsky, "Northern Cheyenne Tribe at a Crossroads: To Develop Coal or Not?" *Wildlife Promise,* September 13, 2012. http://blog.nwf.org/2012/09/northern-cheyenne-tribe-at-a-crossroads-to-develop-coal-or-not/

3. Gayle Perez, "cheyenne-arapaho tribe today." AAA Native Arts, 2008. [please use an updated source]

   http://aaanativearts.com/cheyenne-indians/cheyenne-arapaho-tribe.htm

4. Jason Small, "Guest opinion: Coal development may be key to Northern Cheyenne future." *Billings Gazette*, March 14, 2015.

5. Bonogofsky.

Works Consulted

Andrews, Elaine. *Indians of the Plains.* The First Americans series. New York: Facts On File, 1992.

Axelrod, Alan. *Chronicle of the Indian Wars: From Colonial Times to Wounded Knee.* New York: Prentice Hall General Reference, 1993.

Bonogofsky, Alexis. "Northern Cheyenne Tribe at a Crossroads: To Develop Coal or Not?" *Wildlife Promise,* September 13, 2012. http://blog.nwf.org/2012/09/northern-cheyenne-tribe-at-a-crossroads-to-develop-coal-or-not/

Chief Dull Knife College. *We, The Northern Cheyenne People: Our Land, Our History, Our Culture.* Lame Deer, MT: Chief Dull Knife College, 2008.

Editors of Time-Life Books. *War for the Plains.* The American Indians series. Alexandria, VA: Time-Life Books, 1994. ——. *Tribes of the Southern Plains.* The American Indians series. Alexandria, VA: Time-Life Books, 1995.

Grant, Bruce. *Concise Encyclopedia of the American Indian.* Rev. Ed. New York: Wings Books, 1994.

Grinnell, George Bird. *The Fighting Cheyennes.* North Deighton, MA: JG Press, 1995.

Hirschfelder, Arlene, and Paulette Molin. *The Encyclopedia of Native American Religions.* New York: MJF Books, 1992.

Hoxie, Frederick E., editor. *Encyclopedia of North American Indians.* Boston: Houghton Mifflin Company, 1996.

John Stands in Timber. "Cheyenne Memories." 2011. http://www.cheyennenation.com/memories.html

Josephy, Alvin M., Jr. *500 Nations: An Illustrated History of North American Indians.* New York: Alfred A. Knopf, 1994.

Milner, Clyde A., II, Carol A. O'Connor, and Martha A. Sandweiss, editors. *The Oxford History of the American West.* New York: Oxford University Press, 1994.

Paterek, Josephine. *Encyclopedia of American Indian* Costume. New York: W. W. Norton & Company, 1994.

Perez, Gayle. "Cheyenne-Arapaho Tribe Today." AAA Native Arts, 2008. http://aaanativearts.com/cheyenne-indians/cheyenne-arapaho-tribe.htm

Robinson, Charles M., III. *A Good Year to Die: The Story of the Great Sioux War.* New York: Random House, 1995.

Sandoz, Mari. *Cheyenne Autumn.* Lincoln, NE: Universitry of Nebraska Press, 1992.

Small, Jason. "Guest opinion: Coal development may be key to Northern Cheyenne future." *Billings Gazette,* March 14, 2015. http://usatoday30.usatoday.com/money/industries/energy/2009-03-03-reservation_N.htm

Terrell, John Upton. *American Indian Almanac.* New York: Barnes & Noble Books, 1994.

Utley, Robert M. *The Indian Frontier of the American West 1846–1890.* Albuquerque: University of New Mexico Press, 1993.

Utley, Robert M., and Wilcomb E. Washburn. *The American Heritage History of the Indian Wars.* New York: Barnes & Noble Books, 1992.

Waldman, Carl. *Word Dance: The Language of Native American Culture.* New York: Facts On File, 1994.

Books

Cunningham, Kevin, and Peter Benoit. *The Cheyenne.* True Books: American Indians. New York: Scholastic, 2011.

Santella, Andrew. *Plains Indians.* North Mankato, MN: Heinemann-Raintree, 2012.

Saxena, Shalini. *The Cheyenne People.* Native American Culture series. New York: Gareth Stevens Publishing, 2015.

Tieck, Sarah. *Cheyenne.* Edina, MN: Abdo Publishing Company, 2014.

On the Internet

Native Americans. "The Cheyenne: Native Americans in Olden Times for Kids."

http://nativeamericans.mrdonn.org/plains/cheyenne.html

Native Languages of the Americas. "Native American Facts for Kids: Cheyenne Tribe."

http://www.bigorrin.org/cheyenne_kids.htm

Yellowman, Gordon, Sr. "Sweet Medicine." Wisdom of the Elders.

http://wisdomoftheelders.org/turtle-island-storyteller-gordon-yellowman-sr/

assimilate (ah-SIM-eh-layt)—To absorb into the body or into a group, system, or culture.

casualty (KAZ-yool-tee)—A person killed or injured in a war or accident.

dysentery (DIS-en-tayr-ee)—A disease with inflammation of the intestines, causing diarrhea.

exterminate (ek-ster-mih-nayt)—To wipe out or kill off completely.

fraternal (fruh-TUR-nul)—Of a brother or brothers.

heritage (HAYR-ih-tij)—Values or traditions passed from earlier generations; property that may be or has been inherited.

howitzer (HOW-it-ser)—A short gun for firing shells at a high angle of elevation and low velocities.

incessant (in-SES-unt)—Unceasing; continually repeated.

jurisdiction (joor-is-DIK-shun)—Authority to interpret and apply the law; the extent or territory over which legal or other power extends.

linguistic (ling-GWIS-tik)—Of language.

pemmican (PEM-eh-kin)—North American Indian cake of dried and pounded meat mixed with melted fat.

pristine (pris-TEEN)—In its original and unspoiled condition; fresh, as if new.

regiment (REJ-eh-ment)—A military unit of ground forces organized into two or more battalions (large groups).

ritual (RIT-choo-ul)—The series of actions used in a religious or other ceremony.

sedentary (SED-en-tayr-ee)—Spending much time seated; permanently attached.

MEET THE
AUTHOR

Earle Rice Jr. is a former senior design engineer and technical writer in the aerospace, electronic-defense, and nuclear industries. He has devoted full time to his writing since 1993 and is the author of more than seventy published books. Earle is listed in *Who's Who in America* and is a member of the Society of Children's Book Writers and Illustrators, the League of World War I Aviation Historians, the Air Force Association, and the Disabled American Veterans.